# A FAMILY FOR ZOYA

## THE TRUE STORY OF AN ENDANGERED CUB

Written by Debra Kim Wolf
Illustrated by Annalisa Durante and Marina Durante

Platypus Media, LLC
Washington, D.C.

To the caretakers, veterinarians, and zoo staff who saved and raised Zoya—including Jen Robertson, Eddie Witte, Mandi Sorenson, Jennifer D'Agostino, Gretchen Cole, Andrea Johnson, and more—with special thanks to Gillian Lang for her photography, and to my parents for inspiring my curiosity and energy.

**—Debra Kim Wolf**

To my son, Jacopo. When he was a child we spent a lot of time together drawing animals and tigers were his favourites, now he is a great artist.

**—Annalisa Durante**

To my two cats: Trilli, a rescue cat who was found abandoned when she was very small, and Giottino, a delightful orange kitten who helped me better understand felines. A special thanks to the vets, zookeepers, and adoptive mother of Zoya, Lola, who ensured a happy end to the story.

**—Marina Durante**

# A Note From the Author

**Have you ever visited a zoo? Do you have a favorite zoo animal?
Have you ever wondered where that animal came from or who its family was?**

My favorite animal is the tiger. That's why I wanted to tell the story of Zoya, a rare tiger cub born at the Philadelphia Zoo. Rejected by her mother, Zoya was the lone survivor from a litter of five. Keeping this little endangered Amur tiger alive and healthy was important for her whole species.

But the precious cub didn't just survive—she thrived despite the odds. She was moved to a strange new zoo halfway across the country, became the first cub ever successfully adopted by a different type of tiger, and went on to become a wonderful mother herself.

Those things alone make this a tale worth telling, but Zoya's story also focuses on the people who care and how they make a difference. There's no doubt that humans have hurt tiger populations. Destroying the forests where tigers live, hunting them for their fur or body parts, and even human-caused climate change present big challenges for tiger survival. It might sound like there's no hope or that nothing you do will matter. But that's not true! Many people care deeply about tigers and are working hard to protect them.

Conservationists are passing laws to stop tiger hunting, restoring forests where tigers live, and using modern zoos to learn more about how to save endangered species. Because of these efforts, the number of Amur tigers in the wild has grown from fewer than 50 a few decades ago to almost 400 today. Isn't that amazing?

As you read this book, I hope you'll see a deeper message: Zoya's story celebrates the power of care and compassion—whether it's people helping tigers or a tiger mother embracing a cub that isn't her own. Zoya's journey reminds us that small acts of kindness, for animals or people, can make a big difference.

*Debra Kim Wolf*

**A Family for Zoya: The True Story of an Endangered Cub**

Hardcover first edition • July 2025 • ISBN: 978-1-951995-29-4
eBook first edition • July 2025 • ISBN: 978-1-951995-30-0

Written by Debra Kim Wolf, Text © 2025
Illustrated by Annalisa Durante and Marina Durante, Illustrations © 2025
Project Manager, Cover and Book Design: Violet Antonick, Washington, D.C.
Editors: Hannah Thelen, Washington, D.C.
      Skyler Kaczmarczyk, Washington, D.C.
Editorial Assistants: Daryn Schvimmer, Gweneth Kozlowski, and Sudeeksha Dasari

Spanish edition coming soon.

Teacher's Guide available at the Educational Resources page of PlatypusMedia.com.

Published in the United States by:
Platypus Media, LLC
    750 First Street NE, Suite 700
    Washington, DC 20002
    (202) 546-1674
    Info@PlatypusMedia.com • PlatypusMedia.com

Distributed to the book trade by:
   Baker & Taylor Publisher Services (North America)
      Toll-free: (888) 814-0208
      Orders@btpubservices.com • Btpubservices.com

Library of Congress Control Number: 2024951785

10 9 8 7 6 5 4 3 2 1

Schools, libraries, government, and non-profit organizations can receive bulk discounts.
Contact us at the address above or email us at Info@PlatypusMedia.com

The front cover may be reproduced freely, without modification, for review or non-commercial educational purposes.

All rights reserved. No part of this book may be reproduced in any form without the express written permission of the publisher. Front cover exempted (see above).

Printed in China.

In a cozy den in the Philadelphia Zoo, newborn Zoya let out a tiny whine. **Mew mew**! She was so hungry. But her mother, Koosaka, turned away and wouldn't feed her.

🐾 **Did you know?** Zoya is a rare Amur tiger (they used to be called "Siberian" tigers). Thousands of these huge cats once roamed the frozen ground and dark forests of Russia and Northern China. Now only a few hundred are left in the wild, and many are sick.

Zoya didn't understand that first-time tiger mothers sometimes don't know how to take good care of their babies.

🐾 **Did you know?** The zookeepers hoped that Koosaka would care for her babies, but she wasn't interested.

Zoya's little stomach rumbled. She felt weak. At last, the zookeepers gently lifted her and wrapped her in a fuzzy blanket. They took turns feeding her from a bottle.

The milk tasted good.

Zoya drank eagerly.

But she missed her mother's smell and warm, snuggly fur.

🐾 **Did you know?** Zoya was one of five cubs, but sadly, her four siblings didn't survive long after they were born. To bring a bit of good luck, the zookeepers named the surviving cub Zoya, which means "life" in Russian.

The zookeepers wondered if they could find another tiger mom for Zoya. Then they heard about a tiger named Lola, who lived in a zoo over 1,300 miles (2,100 km) away. She had given birth to three cubs just a day before Zoya was born!

This tiger mom was very good at taking care of her babies.

Could she take care of Zoya, too?

But tiger mothers hardly ever accept cubs who are not their own. And to make things even trickier, Lola and Zoya were *different types* of tigers.

Fostering between different kinds of tigers had never been successful before!

🐾 **Did you know?** There are many types of tigers from different parts of the world. Some are dark and small, like Lola, whose ancestors came from the steamy jungles of Sumatra, in Indonesia. Others, like Zoya, have pale, fluffy fur and grow to be huge; their ancestors came from snowy places in Russia.

The zookeepers had no idea if their adoption plan would work. But they knew it was Zoya's only chance to be part of a tiger family. So they packed her bottle and blanket, gently placed her in a crate, and started on a cross-country journey.

🐾 **Did you know?** Other animals, such as golden retriever dogs, can sometimes care for tiger cubs, but only while they're nursing. Could the zookeepers raise Zoya themselves? Maybe. But tigers raised by humans often have trouble having babies or knowing how to take care of them.

Zoya was only ten days old and the size of a squirrel. Her eyes hadn't opened yet, but she heard the station wagon's rumble and felt the strange **whoosh** of the engine as it raced down the highway toward the Oklahoma City Zoo & Botanical Garden.

🐾 **Did you know?** Newborn cubs have touch, smell, and taste, but they are born with their eyes shut and ear canals closed. During the first week, they are blind and deaf; then, during their second week of life, their eyes and ears open and they can use all five senses.

At rest areas, while other people stopped for snacks, Zoya guzzled a warm bottle of milk. Then she settled back on her fuzzy blanket.

🐾 **Did you know?** After Zoya was fed, the zookeepers encouraged her go to the bathroom by taking a warm rag and patting her butt. This mimics how, in the wild, a mother tiger licks her cubs' behinds until they poop. A tiger mom will then eat the poop to hide her cubs' scent from predators.

After the 22-hour journey, they arrived in Oklahoma.

The zookeepers waited until Mother Lola left her babies for a few minutes to go outside. They then snuck into the den with Zoya.

Zoya's soft fur prickled as they gently rubbed her with straw to disguise her unfamiliar smell. Then they rubbed Mother Lola's three wiggly cubs on Zoya so she would share their scent.

🐾 **Did you know?** Tigers smell like buttered popcorn. This scent comes from their pee and helps them mark their territory, warning any intruders to stay away.

Zoya didn't understand what was happening.

Who were those other **_mew mews_** coming from?

Why did this place smell so different?

And, most importantly, where was her blanket?

Outside the den, Mother Lola finished her lunch and stood impatiently by the door. She wanted to check on her baby boys. The zookeeper slid open the metal divider, and Lola stepped inside.

She stood over Zoya for a long moment. There used to be three cubs. Now there were *four*!

Lola sniffed Zoya as she lay on the floor.

The brothers listened.

🐾 **Did you know?** Because this had never been done before, the zookeepers had no way of knowing how Lola would react. When they first introduced Zoya, the zookeepers carefully watched the video monitor in case Lola rejected the little cub or tried to harm her.

Hot breath covered Zoya's face. Then she felt a big wet tongue licking and nuzzling her all over. How good that felt after her long trip to this strange new place. Zoya chuffed happily.

🐾 **Did you know?** Chuffing is a big cat's way of purring! They blow air through their noses while keeping their mouths closed.

But there was a problem.

While the boys suckled, Zoya lay on the den floor, waiting to be fed.

Hours passed.

Where was her bottle?

She was so hungry!

Was there something she needed to do?

Luckily, Lola was a great mom. She noticed Zoya wasn't nursing and nudged her foster baby closer.

At last, Zoya smelled the milk and suddenly knew what to do. She looked up at her mother with newly opened eyes. Then she nestled next to her brothers and suckled the yummy milk. Warm and safe, she fell asleep with her little belly full.

🐾 **Did you know?** Since Lola had previously been feeding three little ones, veterinarians were concerned that she might not have enough milk to feed four. Every day, they carefully weighed the cubs and were relieved to find that all four baby tigers were gaining weight.

In the beginning, Zoya and her brothers stayed in their den. They wrestled, pounced, nursed, and napped. People could watch them playing and bonding at any time of the night or day on the zoo's tiger cub livestream.

When the cubs were old enough to go outside, they played chase and hunt. These games taught the young tigers the life skills they would need.

The brothers didn't mind that their adopted sister was gentler and didn't roughhouse like they did, or that she was friendlier to the zookeepers.

They didn't care that her stripes were lighter and her fur was shaggier.

🐾 **Did you know?** Like other Amur tigers, Zoya was calmer and gentler than her rowdy Sumatran brothers. When a zookeeper approached, only Zoya barked a friendly *chuff*.

Before long, Zoya grew larger than her brothers. She even grew as large as Mother Lola! But that didn't change how they felt about each other. Despite their differences, they had become a real, loving family.

The day came when Zoya was finally old enough to move somewhere new and start a family of her own.

🐾 **Did you know?** Two of Zoya's brothers were moved to new zoos as well, following recommendations in the Species Survival Plan for Sumatran tigers.

Zoya and Mother Lola stood together by the waterfall and enjoyed their last days in each other's company.

The zookeeper guided Zoya to her crate. She lay quietly as the van raced down the highway.

The last time she traveled had been to meet her new family.

Where was she headed this time?

The trip took over 16 hours, but she finally arrived at the Roosevelt Park Zoo in snowy North Dakota. The tiger enclosure had catwalks where she could roam and an icy waterfall where she could swim.

Even better, the zoo was home to Viktor, a 10-year-old male tiger who was an Amur, the same kind of tiger as Zoya.

Just as the zookeepers hoped, Zoya liked Viktor—a lot.

**🐾 Did you know?** Zoya's move to the new zoo was recommended in the Species Survival Plan for Amur tigers. The zookeepers hoped that Viktor and Zoya would breed, helping to boost the Amur tiger population.

Before long, there was wonderful news: Zoya had given birth to a litter of three healthy cubs—two sweet boys and an adorable girl!

From one side of the country to another, Zoya had been on quite the adventure.

Though she started her journey as a lonely little cub, her adoptive mother, Lola, had shown her how to be a good tiger mother.

Now Zoya knew just how to love and care for her own babies.

***Baby Zoya Being Bottle Fed**** photo by the Philadelphia Zoo*

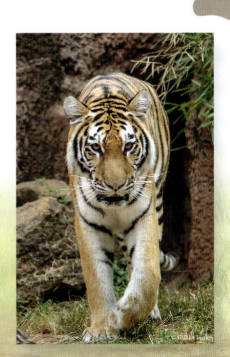

***Teenage Zoya at OKC Zoo**** photo by Gillian Lang*

# Zoya's Story

Zoya was born at the Philadelphia Zoo on July 10, 2017. She was part of a crucial breeding program aimed at strengthening the wild tiger population. From a litter of five rare Amur cubs, Zoya was the only survivor. Sadly, two siblings were stillborn, one died of an injury, and one did not recover after getting sick. After first-time mother Koosaka rejected her, zookeepers bottle-fed Zoya around the clock. Knowing how important it was for Zoya to bond with other tigers, the keepers were hopeful when they learned that a Sumatran tiger at the Oklahoma City Zoo had given birth to triplets just a day before Zoya was born.

Tigers rarely adopt cubs that are not their own, and cross-fostering between different subspecies had never been done successfully before. Despite the odds, Zoya found a loving new family. As you know, she thrived and became a proud mother in March 2022, giving birth to Viktoria, Luka, and Dmitri. Her cubs may one day contribute fresh Amur genes to wild tigers.

Zoya's remarkable journey gained widespread attention, appearing on television and in *People* magazine, inspiring countless individuals with her story of survival and finding family.

**Debra Kim Wolf** is a land conservation attorney (as Debra Wolf Goldstein), award-winning songwriter, and tree hugger. She served on Philadelphia's Fairmount Park Commission and co-founded the Philadelphia Environmental Film Festival. She directs One Little Earth, a nonprofit supporting outdoor programs, films, and books to inspire young nature lovers. She received PennFuture's "Woman of Lifetime Achievement in Conservation" award. The mother of two grown children, she lives in the Philadelphia area with her husband and spunky cockapoo. Toby, a stuffed tiger cub, was her favorite childhood toy. She can be reached at Debra.Kim.Wolf@PlatypusMedia.com.

*The author is donating 100% of her profits to the Tiger Conservation Campaign.*

**Annalisa and Marina Durante** are twin sisters who work together on nature and science illustrations. Marina loves drawing, photography, deep-water diving, and hiking. Her nature photos inspire their art and help her study the scientific details of animals and plants. She hopes their art captures the true beauty of the Earth. Annalisa's curiosity is delicate, and her exploration intimate. She is inspired by her interest in Eastern Philosophy. "Through the Western culture, I learned skills; from the Eastern, inner silence, the base of true listening and meeting with every creature." They have earned awards in naturalistic illustration and have been published widely. They live in Milan, Italy.

# MORE ABOUT AMUR TIGERS

- Tigers are the largest cat species on the planet, and Amurs are the biggest of all! Males measure 9.5-12 feet (2.9-3.7 meters) long and weigh up to 700 pounds (317.5 kilograms). Females are up to 9 feet (2.7 meters) long and weigh up to 370 pounds (168 kilograms). Sumatran tigers like Lola and Zoya's brothers are the smallest subspecies; males weigh only about half of what Amurs do (approximately 350 pounds/159 kilograms).

- Tiger stripes provide camouflage, but it's not just their fur that's striped. If you shave off a tiger's fur, its skin will show the same stripes.

- Each tiger has a unique stripe pattern in the same way human fingerprints are unique to each person. A common method to tell tigers apart from one another is to look at the stripe pattern above each tiger's eyes.

- In the wild, tigers hunt at night, chasing down deer, elk, and wild boar. In short sprints, they can run about 50 mph (80 km/h). Their sharp claws grip the ground and help push them forward. They are also great swimmers who can cross wide rivers.

- Amurs' large paws act like snowshoes to help them move through deep snow.

- 🐾 The typical litter size is three cubs. When tigers are born, they weigh as much as nine oranges, about 2-3 lbs (0.9-1.4 kg). Cubs grow four times larger during their first month! By the time they are four months old, they are as large as a medium-sized dog.

- 🐾 A female tiger typically has four teats arranged in two parallel rows on her underside. Cubs only drink their mother's milk for the first two months but continue to suckle for up to six months.

- 🐾 Tiger cubs have predators such as snakes, crocodiles, and hyenas (about half of wild tiger cubs don't survive past two years old), while humans are the only real predators of adult tigers.

- 🐾 The main threats to tigers are illegal hunting and habitat destruction due to humans cutting down trees to build roads and villages.

- 🐾 Life expectancy of an Amur tiger is 10-15 years in the wild; 16-22 years in human care.

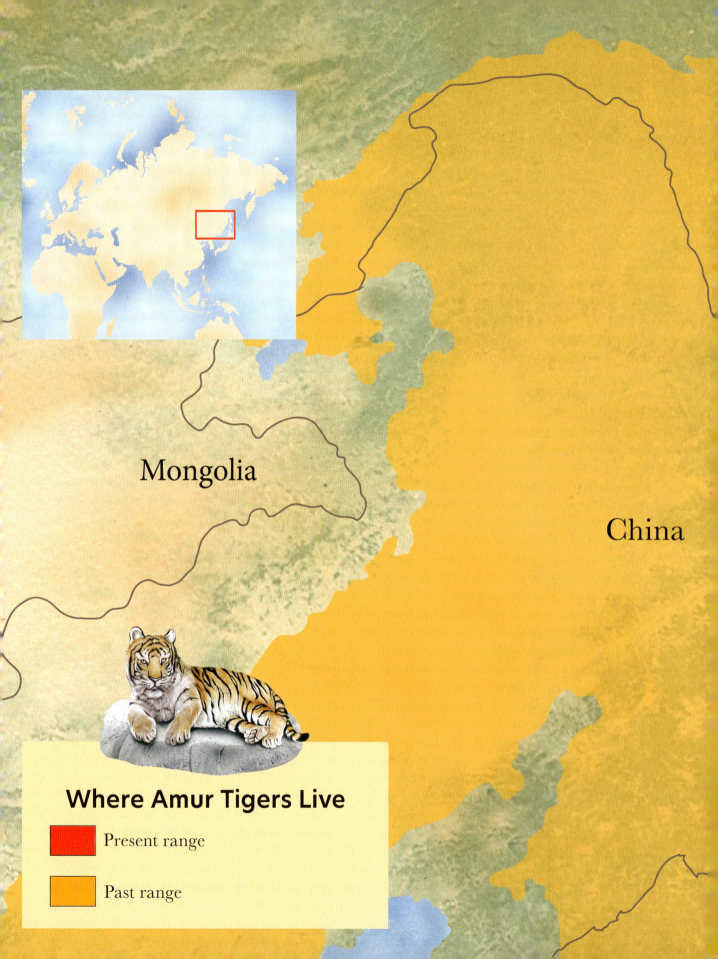

# What is the Amur Tiger Species Survival Plan®?

Amurs, once called "Siberian" tigers, were almost extinct in the wild by the 1940s. Vast areas of their forests were cut down for lumber. They were hunted for their skin and bones, used in traditional medicine. **So few tigers were left that they were renamed "Amur" tigers for the small area of Siberia—the Amur River Valley—where they still live**.

Scientists and conservation organizations from many countries worked together to help. They passed a ban on tiger hunting, created wildlife preserves, and came up with ways to reduce poaching and illegal clearcutting of forests. Slowly, the number of wild tigers increased. Today, there are about 450 Amurs in the wild, with about the same number in zoos. But Amur tigers (and Sumatrans, too) are still considered "critically endangered," the highest threat level. Sadly, Amurs and Sumatrans are not the only types of tigers facing extinction. **In the last 100 years, four of the nine tiger subspecies have disappeared from the wild**.

Because the population of wild Amurs is so small, they suffer from low genetic diversity. This makes it harder for them to adapt to changes in their environment or fight off new diseases. A small population also means fewer possible mates; in that case, individuals may all become related, making their babies unhealthy.

Top zoos accredited by the Association of Zoos & Aquariums created the **Amur Tiger Species Survival Plan** to help. The plan contains breeding recommendations to produce zoo cubs with diverse, fresh genes that can one day be introduced into the wild tiger population to make them healthier.

This is called "genetic rescue." Zoya and her siblings were bred and born as part of this plan, which also includes a Tiger Conservation Campaign to reduce poaching and help neighboring villagers build tiger-proof pens for their farm animals.